FROM COCOA BEANS TO CHOCOLATE

BY BRIDGET HEOS · ILLUSTRATED BY STEPHANIE FIZER COLEMAN

AMICUS ILLUSTRATED and **AMICUS INK**
are published by Amicus
P.O. Box 1329, Mankato, MN 56002
www.amicuspublishing.us

**LIBRARY OF CONGRESS
CATALOGING-IN-PUBLICATION DATA**
Names: Heos, Bridget, author. | Coleman, Stephanie Fizer,
    illustrator. | Heos, Bridget. Who made my lunch?
Title: From cocoa beans to chocolate / by Bridget Heos ;
    illustrated by Stephanie Fizer Coleman.
Description: Mankato, MN : Amicus, [2018] | Series: Who
    made my lunch?
Identifiers: LCCN 2016054919 (print) | LCCN 2016056909
    (ebook) | ISBN 9781681511207 (library binding) | ISBN
    9781681512105 (e-book) | ISBN 9781681521459 (pbk.)
Subjects: LCSH: Chocolate processing—Juvenile literature.
    | Cocoa processing—Juvenile literature. | Chocolate—
    Juvenile literature.
Classification: LCC TP640 .H46 2018 (print) | LCC TP640
    (ebook) | DDC 664/.5—dc23
LC record available at https://lccn.loc.gov/2016054919

EDITOR: Rebecca Glaser
DESIGNER: Kathleen Petelinsek

Printed in the United States of America
HC 10 9 8 7 6 5 4 3 2
PB 10 9 8 7 6 5 4 3 2 1

ABOUT THE AUTHOR

Bridget Heos is the author of more than
80 books for children. She lives in Kansas City
with her husband and four children, all of whom
like chocolate.

ABOUT THE ILLUSTRATOR

Stephanie Fizer Coleman is an illustrator, tea
drinker, and picky eater from West Virginia, where
she lives with her husband and two silly dogs. When
she's not drawing, she's getting her hands dirty in the
garden or making messes in the kitchen.

Mmm . . . chocolate. A delicious and ready-to-eat treat! But what if you had to make that chocolate yourself? You would need to grow the main ingredient: cocoa beans!

Cocoa beans are grown near the equator, where it is warm all year. Grab your passport! Most cocoa is grown on small farms in West Africa and South America.

Sadly, many children do work on cocoa farms for little or no pay.
But Fair Trade farms like this one in Africa do not allow child labor.
The cocoa farmers will show you around, though.

Cocoa beans grow in large green pods. The beans are the seeds of the fruit. From these seeds, cocoa trees grow. This tree was planted three years ago. Now it is producing fruit.

The fruit ripens in about five months. When it turns yellow, it's time to harvest. Here in Africa, that happens in October. Use a long stick with a knife at the end to cut down the fruit. Careful! When you have a basket full, carry it to another group of workers. They will remove the seeds.

First, they split open the fruit by beating it with clubs or knives. Then they separate the seeds from the pulp.

Later, the seeds are covered with leaves from banana trees. This turns the seeds brown.

Next, spread the seeds on a mat in the sun. When they dry, pour them into bags. They are now called cocoa beans.

Sell them to a chocolate maker. Now, the cocoa
beans will travel on a ship to the factory.

Put on your hairnet and apron. You now work at a small chocolate factory. It smells delicious! Here, some work is done by hand, and some is done by machine. Sort the cocoa beans, and pick out any imperfect ones.

CAUTION!
HOT

Now roast the cocoa beans in the oven.

This adds flavor and loosens the shell.

Pour the roasted beans into the cracker. This machine cracks the beans and separates the husks from the nibs inside.

The nibs go into the grinding machine. To make dark chocolate, add sugar only. For milk chocolate, add sugar *and* milk powder. More waiting: the chocolate must be ground for up to three days!

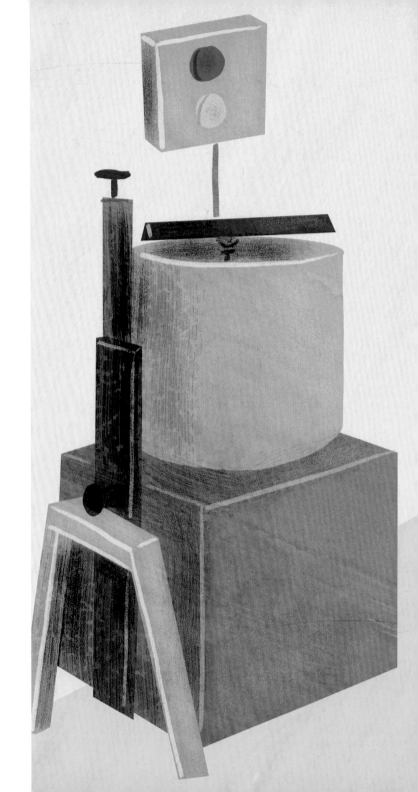

A different machine will heat and cool the chocolate several times. This is called tempering. Without this step, the chocolate bar would be crumbly and dull.

Pour the shiny chocolate into molds. As the bars harden, they shrink. They easily tip out of the molds. Wrap each bar—now people can buy them!

Thanks to the farmer, the harvest workers,
and the chocolate factory workers, you have
a chocolate bar to eat with your lunch. Yum!

WHERE ARE COCOA BEANS GROWN?

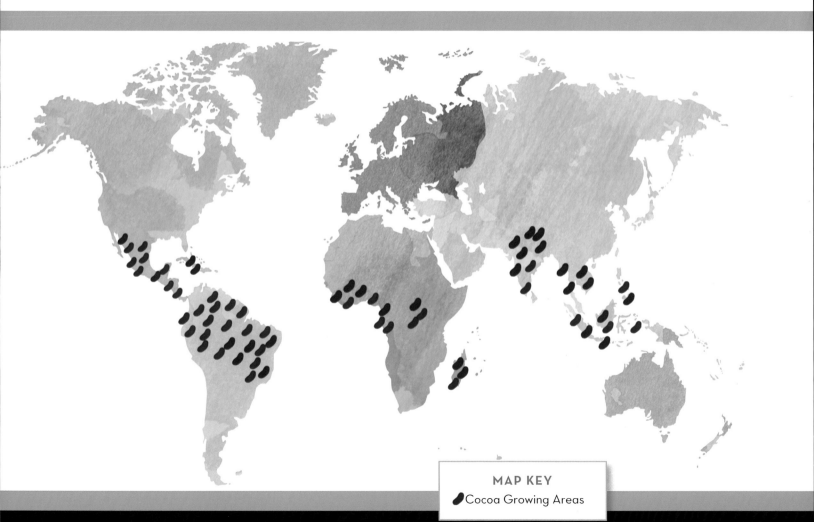

MAP KEY

Cocoa Growing Areas

GLOSSARY

cocoa bean The seed of a cocoa plant.

dark chocolate Candy made from ground cocoa beans and sugar.

Fair Trade farm A farm on which workers are paid a fair price for their crops and treated fairly; for example, child labor is not allowed.

husk The outer layer of a cocoa bean.

milk chocolate Candy made from ground cocoa beans, sugar, and milk.

nib The inner portion of a cocoa bean.

pulp The soft and juicy part of a fruit.

tempering The process of heating and cooling chocolate to make it smoother.

WEBSITES

All About Chocolate: Just for Kids
http://archive.fieldmuseum.org/chocolate/kids.html
Learn about how chocolate is made and "make" your own virtual chocolate online.

Equal Exchange: From Bean to Bar
http://equalexchange.coop/products/chocolate/steps
This fair trade organization shows photos of cocoa bean harvesting.

The Science of Chocolate Facts for Kids
http://easyscienceforkids.com/the-science-of-chocolate-facts-for-kids-video/
Watch this video to learn about the science of making chocolate.

Every effort has been made to ensure that these websites are appropriate for children. However, because of the nature of the Internet, it is impossible to guarantee that these sites will remain active indefinitely or that their contents will not be altered.

READ MORE

Herrington, Lisa. *Beans to Chocolate*. New York: Children's Press, 2013.

Nelson, Robin. *From Cocoa Bean to Chocolate*. Minneapolis: Lerner, 2013.

Stewart, Melissa, and Allen Young. *No Monkeys, No Chocolate*. Watertown, Mass.: Charlesbridge, 2013.